LAST NIGHT IN EDEN

The Sonnets

PALMETTO
PUBLISHING
Charleston, SC
www.PalmettoPublishing.com

© 2024 by J. Harold Ryder

Hardcover ISBN: 979-8-8229-4529-6
Paperback ISBN: 979-8-8229-4530-2
eBook ISBN: 979-8-8229-4531-9

LAST NIGHT IN EDEN
The Sonnets

J. HAROLD RYDER

For Susie
My first and immortal muse

Pulvis es et pulverem reverteris

Genesis 3:19

Ad majorem Dei gloriam

"Life's but a walking shadow."

Macbeth

Shakespeare

Sometimes In Springtime

Sometimes in springtime buds too soon do bloom,
Before winter's spent, her cold blood is through;
When hearts hopeful, flood, then gushing assume,
For lilac scent spent is the April rush due—
"By degrees, everything!" (that's what you told me)
Noting how even the moon on us crept;
When seeing a sliver you got up to hold me,
Too late by then love I'd already leapt.
Still, to this day I visit the place
On occasion, if only to see your sweet face;
But by now (I'm convinced), some other tips trace
Your lips for my loss, my soul's sad disgrace.
But what to do, now? What might I do here?
Now that the ocean for drowning is sheer.

Still Drunk On Your Lungs

Still drunk on your lungs I staggered the night,
Through until street lamps and stars struck me sober;
Then in the black light, the heart of my plight,
I saw you above me in tall grass and clover.
May I tell you already how my time is spent?
Away from your bosom, in hell silent hushed?
Resigned, to just thought, and memory pent,
Candles burn only where your soul was touched.
Insomuch as I can, my heart I release,
Every chance in a lifetime of bliss;
Where if not for your breast, I'd already cease
To exist for that night in the garden, the kiss.
When dust, for sweet dust, we one moment shared,
Then left for tomorrow with more knowledge, paired.

When A Cold Constant Rain

When a cold, constant rain can stone even carve,
Trenches in granite through valleys and plains;
Then what chance, this cheek, cherry we crave,
Fragile for blushing then clouds come with stains.
Follow now those blue streams that to her heart lead,
First fount, and lusty that is Beauty's start;
What that hot spring, wets, is nothing if deed
Leaves only rank weeds when two islands part.
But back that surface, calm, cold to stare,
And see what other cheek blushing there waits;
What fair nature blest, death comes to make rare,
That flower bled out and pale for what hates.
Yourself, Beauty's rose, you see in that water,
And deeper, tomorrow; that is Beauty's daughter.

As Much As I Love Thee

As much as I love thee I loathe thee the more,
To see so much warmth in spring go to waste;
Then in few short moons, what all eyes adore,
Goes to beauty's doom, still frozen, still chaste.
Sapphire blue streams, that to hotter source flow,
In white regal wrist now your pure beauty show;
But what then, when death, with winter wind comes,
To freeze beauty's fountain, make ice from our wombs.
But should Beauty's womb give to Beauty back,
What was her store given then all eyes are pleased;
To see selfsame, wealth, eyes bright and hair black,
Then your love lives on when we're all deceased.
Making you, Beauty's bank, that pure beauty stored,
But dead and gone are a desert abhorred.

Might I Finally Now

Might I finally, now, my lover compare,
To that one month—the fourth? God knows she's
as fair;
And in that, her lung, is April's own air,
And in that fresh cheek is a red rose as rare.
In Maytime the buds for their blood too tight cling,
Then fall in the front of June—flowers to feel;
Sometimes, in autumn the birds sweeter sing,
Then comes a cold breeze, to heart wound congeal.
But just as that month, so too is my love
Too brief, when in four swift weeks she is gone;
Come May, then and June, with nothing to move,
September sees two stems, soon snow on the lawn.
And her cheek, that once did my palm brush and hold,
For winter freezing is still red but cold.

So Now Are My Songs

So now are my songs for my star, all the same,
That in each one might one find here her name;
Or, if not here, then in my Muse's flame,
Born to burn hotter beyond my own fame.
Charge me thus, in my youth your bright torch I held,
When you,—too near me for fear did not tell;
The flame, though a shield, the wax only swelled
My heart at that spot, the plot where I fell.
This torch that I speak of I only can keep,
As long as you, Muse, return a good fire;
And just when you thought it: my heart was too deep,
For your eyeballs only I kept my sight higher—
Au contraire, mon chéri! that mirror I broke,
That second I heard you, when you looked, spoke.

And It Happens

And it happens, each time—first love the same
When eyes, into eyes tender Love's fragile flame;
That first breath, before, when come sacred name,
Then life by next night for sight, never tame.
From first sight, those fires, to brow above move
By now (one for fear) of love's slightly raised;
Then on to the cheek, whose blush love can prove
If not for one reason that blood is amazed.
From there, to the chin, that tremoring quite
For that jaw, that to touch—(now follow this line);
Those soft downy, strings, upon earlobe white,
That if cherry red, that's surely a sign.
Where back, to that start, where all this began:
Those torches that teach that heaven should ban.

When I See It—And I Do!

When I see it—and I do! how Death justly waits
Patient, not desperate, my breath quick to take;
Whereafter last, night, my eyes from flesh break,
Then rest I shall with light assured of my dates.
But before my bones, are laid out—displayed
With flowers, like lovers, around me arrayed;
With my arms, cold and hard, preposterously posed
That pine box, inside, a stone vault enclosed.
Alas! Before that breeze—final wind blows
Western, my ashes—to where only knows;
My heart hot, bled out, shall outlive that granite,
That white bone beneath with nothing left on it.
Save this: what words I left here, bones above,
My pen is in heaven, to write of my love.

Forgive Me Beforehand

Forgive me beforehand this vow that I make,
If there come with it a phrase I can't keep;
But of love true, I write, until two lips break
Is something for touching with you wet and deep.
But be kind, to that other one (now in
Your breast)—left, that beats beside better thine;
My love—if you want, shall flourish, grow in,
But if not I perish—(and want to) that's fine.
And you know dear by now I'm sure without doubt
Exactly, just where this madness is borne;
What two lips, keep pursed, two other ones pout,
Two parts, alone, turn hotter for scorn.
If what I write, here, is still true tomorrow,
Then I've not lived well, except in sweet sorrow.

Now The Aspens Are Turned

Now the aspens are turned, and with them the hoards,
Of birds, sitting heavy in winter's black bough;
And in it, the sunset, those beams leaning towards,
The west is a whisper for what I lack now.
Once, I did also this dark lady love,
When in my own age of youth (indiscretions);
But her beauty too much, for my words to move,
She left me for his stage, four more questions.
Where the cricket, still chirps, so too is my love
Soft, in the twilight and musk falling on;
Where the nightingale, mourns, my beats slower prove
Life is like death, the heart calling on.
And of them, those asking, who, where, what, when,
The only two left are how and what then.

Since Away You Left

Since away you left in your eyes I have dwelt,
With the best of my days in your dark shadow spent;
The nights, I've endured, the cold reasons felt,
For moaning, till morning alone with your scent.
When first did mine eyes upon beauty lay
Forever, then altered my poor body was;
For beauty, to see it, to love it and say,
What pleasure there is, my own joy because.
But a beautiful face is a moment in time
Whereas, the soul like a diamond lives on;
So my love, for my love, a fire sublime,
Burns for your memory till my heart gives on.
With those rubies, thy lips, now not mine but his,
To that foul phrase, accept: it is what it is.

That Man Dies But Once

That man dies but once I too used to think,
　　When with that last gasp of air he's released;
His sad, long life done, content then to sink,
A cold corpse on earth, a body deceased.
But a death a day, now, my heart must endure,—
By slow cuts, ten thousand or more (I should add);
My lover, to see her, then move on unsure,
What shall of me come, a friend that she had.
Should I live long enough my love to hear say,
Torture she too felt then happy that last;
That breath, like a blade, my heart shall filet,
At least until death, my flesh from here passed
Or if, not, then here deal one more to my heart,
Some things are worse than a death till we part.

Who Doesn't In June

Who doesn't in June that scent love to catch,—
   The rosebud, in full bloom with fragrance to tease;
To sweet petals, soon, that silk unfurled match
To nostrils flared smack and tips tender please.
In mid June, the roses for love perfume lend
But only, for noses that red lips do love;
Then by summer's, end, those lips warmer wend
And die autumn in, no more souls to move.
Thou, that art now in thy sweet summer's height,
O love shouldst that silk, with hands tender share;
Lest by frost come, early, death in cold light, night,
We've no more perfume and you no more air.
All this, the nose knows, the rose fragile grows,
Happy to have it but cry when it goes.

Here, Where Deep Vapors

Here, where deep vapors of love come and stay,
Here, for my heart, vapid—cold as spring clay;
My heart, for your part, I take back sweet thief,
My thorn I keep sharp on stem and green leaf.
I, too—fear those lips, whose lines my lips tempt
To press, no less than those petals that taunt;
And, yet—crimson silk, and wet I once dreamt,
My nights, for that night my head hungry haunt.
And if one, lip to kiss, so much sweet joy brings
Then what, might two do, my garden to see?
Already, for thinking that thorn my hand stings,
Making a bed out of pure ecstasy.
O, steal again! Sweet lips! Tender-most thief,
That from one last kiss, thou endeth my grief.

Then Pray Love Me Meet

Then pray love me meet, that one tree beneath,
Whilst we're yet young and still with our teeth;
In few days, defeat, and then with a breath,
Two candles, one flame—a kiss and our death.
But for it all: the oath and the growth,—
The promise, to love thee until even loathe;
The nup, and the sup, the sharing of cup,
And all that goes with it—(before we wake up).
I shall pack my bag, there, in the mid of light—
Moon, when with it, waning honey drips;
To kiss thee, there once, then call it my night
Good, for your pleasure, the sight of your lips.
Then take heart, dear dove! Though I am not there,
In flesh I still dwell, my spirit—your hair.

At First Brush, Love's Rush

At first brush, Love's rush, why must we decide
Here, friends between and lovers forever?
Why not just let ride? Say three words, never,
Lest by that one breath come two friends that lied.
Still, when you're near me my tongue I must bite
Down, lest by one slip mine own I betray;
Then, by deed done, too young we must lay
Both hearts at Love's door never to fight.
But since it's been leaked, how might I proceed
Now, knowing from palms pressed no going back;
Words, then are swords, till hands cold and slack,
Lovers leave nothing but bosoms to bleed.
Then one of two things, to come at that end:
I gain a new love or keep a sweet friend.

Just As By One Bolt

Just as by one bolt, do bonfires begin,
  Or huge floods, deluges from one tiny drop;
So, too—tender love, from one look, that's sin,
To steal—virgin bud then the full blossom lop.
Quick kiss me, then, the silver moon under,
Afore morning beams—the dawn knows we left;
Pray press, pilgrim palms, that when breasts asunder,
Hearts keep through daydreams till hands in night deft.
So too, as the twig, today comes the tree
Tomorrow, the same as the wind the wood bent;
My love, in my soul, although I can't see,
Your hand I still have by your flower, your scent.
So powerful, that touch, though light our hearts sever,
By one will we brave it, to wake up never.

For Unlawful Carnal Knowledge

For unlawful carnal knowledge I sleep
Unlucky, in love and in fleeting youth;
Consequently, for blissful pleasure I leap,
Kind to those lips that speak of treasured truth.
But was it a fire, in her eyes that made
My own blind, that, staring into nothing else I see?
Or, by them—those others, features once laid
Comes more sweet gush that some call heavenly.
O, no! It is neither that fire in her eye,
Or, that—her slight smile that slanted causes sighs;
But rather, her fine foot, and quivering thigh,
That my heart beguile, where all my breath lies.
Happy, then in it, that blush (we all know),
Is something we want, but still fear to go.

Or Just As That Student

O r just as that student, afraid—too much
First day, for lessons the long way goes to;
My love, for her scent, her beauty to touch,
I hem and then haw knowing doom is due.
Still careful I go, to her hairstrings play
Hesitant, when music calls for deep tongues;
Those soft, dulcet tones, in heart (I could say)
Are notes for my own sheets, scandalous songs.
O love! If thou art—as they say that fair youth
That, being schooled is my verdure bud tucked;
Then beauty, I learn, and from that your truth,
A flower, like mine untutored, unplucked.
Then, lips, for sweet lips, in night having learned,
Thou art my teacher and kisses I've earned.

I Admit I Did Lie

I admit I did lie when I with my heart,
Did swear by my life I could not love you more;
It's just that some things for time one can't chart,
Stars being masters when head and heart war.
When with a sweet sigh, I see other souls
Throw away what was a lifetime of bliss;
Then question—(I do!) how much night controls
The path of true love from eyesight to kiss.
But nevermind, now, for the world has flipped,
Slipped, from a fair day to flesh and decay;
My foot, for that act, in Love's ocean dipped,
Is subject to more now, and that I can't say.
Except, all that was, is still just the same,
My love for you now is an eternal flame.

When, In November

When, in November, skies gray crying freeze,
And in barren trees, the birds have all flown;
Those leaves, brown and burnt, fall back with ease
And blow west to winter and tombstones unknown.
Time of day, now, when the light well past noon
And the seasons, for reasons unknown have turned;
My eyes eastward gaze, to night harvest moon,
Bulging above fields once golden now burned.
Still look I, do yearning my love's bosom to,
Where rest I, might at last my hard weary head;
If nothing else, tell her, how I loved her too
When wind flesh did shake, and tree leaves did shed.
When in summer, those limbs, do leaves better keep,
Till after November, the scythe's bloody reap.

When To Time I Think On

When to time I think on, the days that do pass,
Each, like a link in a chain until death;
Then the better, it looks, that untrod grass,
Where men no more work, for that rest beneath.
On that wet white silk, my love's warm bed
Could I breathe, my last breath, the sweet air into;
And from this rank, realm, my soul let shed
Where angels are cast, their time here through.
What then would I want, no more pain to feel
Here, where men fret until in earth they're laid;
The world, for its deeds, when born fate we seal
A lot of us, for that first mistake made.
Until, that is when, that one comes to wake,
All those old bones, no more sin to make.

When I Watch Now How Men

When I watch how men for new fads do change,
     How people, with fashions like winds turn and
burn;
With their clothes, one day hot, the next day are strange,
Then again by next year—same threads return.
When I witness those leaves, today green and lush,
With the flowers—though sweet, tomorrow are sour;
How seconds, turn minutes, to stone even crush,
Even hours hands swallow, sands—lands devour.
Then, to my love I do look on with fire
And, sigh, I for beauty that sad cannot stay;
That, useless, my powers—(forget desire),
She keeps my night bright and I her best day.
Then the world, I care not! I look on and laugh,
To see what it thinks, (it knows not her half).

How Often We See it

How often we see it: the flower in its light,
Summer, when joyous the hour to take in;
The perfume, to be it! That bed to wake in,
But for the dread canker, worm in the night.
Can I tell you here now, how the first flower falls?
Its petals, for beauty in morning take flight;
One, by sad one, till no bloom at all,
Then for that churl theft immaculate white.
Since from fair beauty, only that begets
The red rose, to look on we only want more;
Petals, whose sweet silk, the even dew wets,
Then in light unfurled we weep for that bore.
Sweet deed, in first night, by morning deflower,
Turning a sweet bud to weed rank and sour.

Here To Time And Space

Here to time, and space, my lover removed
The miles, from her smile too many to count;
To look, on Earth's face, I see where I loved
Behind, now to think a black hell amount.
O! That I had me a cup of that drink
Cool, and drawn from that spring River Lethe;
Where, my night done, might I slip off and sink,
Where men no more fret and graves sabers sheathe.
And how many, more, I fear here have fallen
My love, from her hand, beauty separated;
They, there—in the ground, dutifully callen,
The wound, by Love's knife dull and serrated.
Then one mile, or million (no matter to me),
Away from those lips is my lips agony.

As It Bends In The Breeze

As it bends in the breeze, so too grows the tree,
A twig, soon a trunk with limbs strong and stout;
So my heart, for your eyes—(sunshine for me),
Forever in debt for that long summer out.
If one kiss, of lips, so much pleasure brings,
Then what might two do, at that heaven's gate?
For what my part's, worth, a thorn better stings,
When petals wetter for waiting abate.
So too as one touch to the tiniest seed
In no time, the rose by morning becomes;
My hands, for your hands, turn towards you and bleed
Until Autumn's close, and winter wind numbs.
Then Love, having won, Death hath no more power,
And what was just words turns to bud forever.

Because Death Comes Like It

Because Death comes like it, that thief in the night,
To swipe precious breath from beauty's red lips;
Should you, Beauty's bud, that graces our sight,
Now double your blood before winter clips.
O vicious decision! when in summer's height,
To see you a blossom with silk red and all;
To want, that last bliss, but then after flight,
Petals left unplucked in autumn still fall.
And what then, when we who of beauty write,
Weep for your bloom in that eternal tomb?
The last one, there out, the lantern's cold light
Step then there with you to Beauty's last womb.
Then Death, once thought black, and foul as the night,
No more comes to reap for our lines in true light.

Tell Me Not How The Rain

Tell me not how the rain and wind here are kind,
When in a few years they all things destroy;
How all beauty, pure, thought for life assigned,
Are washed back to oceans for waves to enjoy.
When witness I am, to the seasons that change
How, in a few short weeks all flowers are gone;—
Even I, on this page, for writing am strange,
Once I am done for my words proven wrong.
But my love that's now in the spring of her youth
Fresh, shall she stay as she now here appears;
That though the rains, come, and with it warm tears,
She keeps her beauty without me for truth.
Such a power, is my verse, to her fragrance make,
Even when winter winds, flowers must take.

Between Double Beds

Between double beds the morning I pace,
Staring, out into the gray breaking dawn;
Where lungs, once did heave, the shadow's embrace
Seems too much for me, the day shaking on.
When to times, my muse for leaving I'm dry,
My night quill—(too often), in Beauty's fount dipped;
When once with Love's thought, my spirit could fly,
For my head's doubt are my wings sudden-clipped.
But whose hands, tonight, are her hands caressing,
I ask my blank palms (naked undressing);
She, has her fountain, some other pulp pressing,
While I've my hot beats, she's his paper blessing.
Until, day it comes, like sweet inspiration,
To dry out the sheets, my worst perspiration.

But Just What Then

But just what then, when, Death for my own comes,
Swift as that breath that a flame fragile outs?
What then, in that earth, the cool of stone tombs,
When bones sleep in peace but souls still have doubts.
Those same sweet warm words, I know you will use
Again, when at that scene one web we weave;
To keep me, in good faith, a wraith for abuse,
Then you in shadows away with him leave.
Then be blunt! When come time my last tie to cut,
No sharp sentence, spare, no phrases with strings;
For those three words, I hate: could, would and but,
They have no worth to me at awkward endings.
When, for my sad sake, you hold your heart back,
You stay a sweet queen and I'm painted black.

Overboard Is My Heart

Overboard is my heart, where drown good I could,
If only to hear those sweet sirens sing;
Breathe deep, here the air! The tempest lewd
Before the last lash, then nothing to sting.
So art thou, my love like steadfast that star,—
Northern, and brightest that guides ships at night;
That though, yet above, a torch that is far,
By your sighs left me I keep my sails tight.
But love, ask me not how much I thee love,
When for the miles long my lips cannot move;
The bones, in my rack, the jaw in my skull,
But for fear on the shore, other bells toll.
So too, here my soul, like those fires that dim,
To doubt my love now I can't think, to swim.

Not From Birds—Their Flocks

Not from birds—their flocks, do I my news get,
And yet, sometimes by their songs I am sad;
Nor in leaves—tea in cups, is my future set,
Read at the bottom to tell good or bad.
Not in stars—constellations, do I my night chart
Although (I must say), sometimes love predict;
Those orbs, in their paths, strange change and then start
Two hearts, in play as if those bones were picked.
However, in those my lover's bright eyes,
Do I find my way for what fire supplies;
And in those, her hands, and in those her thighs,
Are all my best joy, the source of my sighs.
O, but sweet ends! When tears come from pearls,
The night, for time done, the glint in her curls.

It Happens—And Fast!

It happens—and fast! when least we expect,
Next love, that is when eyes eyes reflect;
Where from one flash, yes, (no more than a second)
Hearts must consent or from that fire abscond;
And if one, sweet beat here by blood can make fire,
Then what might two do, to stoke dark desire.
First love, that oft does by one look begin,
From twain sparks, proceed, to a soul soon in trouble;
If from looks, desire, that first thought is sin,
Bound to a fire feed if that thought is double.
And how does it go? This lust that I speak?—
Each time, it's the same after eyes eyes meet;
From fire, to the name, first word makes us weak,
That no deep ocean can outcome defeat.
Such a heat, by eyes borne, when lungs hellish huff,
Only by lips then and wet cry enough.

Chiding Time, That Only True Constant

Chiding Time, that only true constant I find,
When in the steel-cold silence I wait;
Those sands, in my hands, one by one grind,
Till tired I relent to that patient friend Fate.
That harsh tyrant, Time, down on my flesh bears,
When stand I on shores and gaze on tomorrow;
The warm tide, comes in, and wave by wave wears
On me, till seconds and minutes swallow.
And yet, how happy my soul here surrenders,
When I look back on my love I did love;
Those seconds, all counted, one life that renders
Nothing, if I left my true heart above.
Then that cold clock, that still counts my life with breath,
Has on my bones nothing, that black blanket Death.

A Picture I Keep

A picture I keep from memory made,
That though years have passed still in my mind
hangs;
But with each tear dear, warm, I fear to fade,
To wake up to find alas it is strange.
That once we did meet in a candleless night
When eyes, into eyes, provide only light;
That moment, though sweet, so too shall take flight,
Against all my power, my head's puny might.
But that portrait you painted, is deep in my soul
Seared, and sealed by that kiss therein still;
Where look I on, fond, from morning until
Death quiets my heart, makes my spirit whole.
Where your beauty, with truth paired, forever's framed,
Until I am dead, my heart's tarnish tamed.

What I Would Not Give

What I would not give to lose this strange pain,
  Borne by a gash when my love my way looked;
My love, with each lash, my body is hooked,
Wanting to die for her, all my part's in vain.
But my love, for my love's as a high fever still,
That, when in her sight my brain is on fire;
Or, when away my lungs pant until
My illness is stopped by an ocean's desire.
And what power do you a goddess now have,
That both the disease and ease you control;
Your beauty, a flower, that scent takes a toll
Until by one hour lips wet soothe and salve.
O, but sweet trade! That what causes my illness,
Is the same thing that cures me, when in duress.

Now In That Glass, Gaze

Now in that glass, gaze, to see that face there
Last time! Before for its own time it must leave;
Then, gone—not for good, that last trace we bear
Upon Beauty's bier by your mourners to grieve.
And what can say, better, my black words back up
When I, with my pen have to that faint bourne fled;
Than you—tender muse! These lines I stack up,
Against what I claim, long after I'm dead.
Those readers tomorrow, shall on my lines weep
Deep, to think how such a queen here once breathed;
Then weep, even more, to think those bones wreathed,
This green grass, beneath no more you to keep.
Except, by that breath, should you with me bear,
Your blood beats on not with me but your heir.

Rolling Back, Not The Years

Rolling back, not the years but the tears your youth to,
The pictures I peep on and sigh on that time;
To see you, in sleep—and more your growth through,
The weeks that we kissed, those moons in your prime.
But how many, more, might I say that I left—
Like you, in that warm ground never to bring back;
You there, still were missed, and I was bereft,
Sorry for what I did that night, alack.
O, but that I could by Love's lightest wings,
Be there, where you are—O all for such naught!
Some other, a lover—now for that touch sings,
He got that bloom that I thought was mine, taut.
Sweet lips, sweeter flight, when pressing you make
Perfume tomorrow that nothing can take.

Since Time Now Is Space

Since time now is space, taken with grain
When, backward looking I see all my folly;
My rhyme, your disgrace, to you I'm a stain,
For what flesh did want, my sin you to sully.
That too long away, from you I have been,
That worst sin, committed, I here now confess;
The strange nights, I've kept, the weird visions seen,
When rain meets sunlight and lungs, bosoms bless.
But what might I give to you here to make up?—
What, for my life can I truthfully write?
When others, for less, by those acts break up,
With never, another chance to make right.
But whose pilgrim palms are you now with, praying?
I ask myself as time is decaying.

How Many More, Others

How many more, others, I've wondered and wept
And wept, and wondered for their candles kept;
The debt, there incurred, for having stepped
Then stopped, just short—the night's best depth.
To even this day, that spot having marked,—
In the garden, I harden each time spring nears;
When on that damp clay, before the lark harked,
My jacket I gave you then dried your tears.
But why did he have to come like a cloud?—
Straight away, in the blue to our sky shroud?
I ask myself, each time the same,
Then leave more heat for your cold flame.
Where, this day to, I your warm smile think on,
And your blouse, all wet, the smooth palm pink on.

That My Heart You All Own

That my heart you all own from sun to sun,
　　Should that be enough when your frame I can't have;
But my head? All my thoughts? That I can't fathom,
How you're not my mistress and still I'm your slave.
And what do I tend on, from morn until dusk—
I mean, what, regal power do you have over me?
That I keep you, here sweet, but he has your musk,
And I must rely on pure memory.
And no rest for my head, when my thoughts are done,
I think on those twin lips that feed my desire;
He has your bed, when night has begun,
And I'm just a warm salve for your darker fire.
Until, at least then, you my lover be,
He pleases that half that I never see.

How Many A Time

How many a time I tried in light veiled—
My love, to pen true, her fair beauty paint;
But then, done and sad, to see my lines paled,
To her face with lace, or worse I did taint.
Far better a poet, painter's required,
Now to her features with fine touches capture;
My own hand, thought good, my brush is too tired
For this creature pure, to blush a whole chapter.
True! Better rhymes for her smile I have read,
And, of her eyes on a cold canvas seen;
But, those—for their worth, her lips are more red,
And of that her breast, her heart is pristine.
And of them—those others, now this here listen,
When they're wet at night they glisten.

That Hour Of Love, Now

That hour of love, now, when time hangs and bends,
  About the boughs, barren; those limbs autumn
brings;
As smoke, from new fires, from stacks lifts and lends,
And summer, the last drop of light from night wrings.
Still, how I sigh when I think on those nights,—
Now, for the time gone are ghosts faint and fading;
What love, keeps here hot, is the best of our flights,
Not for fresh air but the snow that is waiting.
No matter, now, for the reasons are different,
Not for me, but for flesh, and more time having thought;
When pursued, and pursuing, we fall for one scent
Then wake up in love when we both ought.
A smoke scent, can do that, a strange season bring,
As aspen leaves, golden, in late summer ring.

O Bittersweet Light!

O bittersweet, light! is love's first leave
  When hands, squeezing tight must fingers release;
Bitter, for tears, salt drops from Love's sieve,—
Sweet, for the memory, pain soon to seize.
When, for my absence is strengthened my love
For that, should that time I call precious yearning;
But for fear, the farther away I move,
What I leave here is sadder returning.
But then in sweet sleep, do my eyes clearer see,
Hearing, your words like the lark at first light:
What love, leaves here sweet, so too it shall be,
The same as when palms pressed palms at last sight.
Then begins it, my journey, to love's compound hip,
Until your true kiss, then sweet makes that trip.

For All Of Your Knowledge

For all of your knowledge, with patience I sleep,
Longing, for that line when flesh crosses over;
To see you, fall too, in heaven too deep,
He has you in light but I am your lover.
But to have you in light is only as good,
As that time allows, your full presence in;
When others, show up, then with thought I brood,
Sulking, in silence—in essence my sin.
But, in the end—it doesn't really matter,
Does it? Last thing I remember hearing;
Then water,—the warm rain, when time is wearing
Thin on the mattress when pearls fall and scatter.
And still, the pain, becomes the garden,
Even as our bodies harden.

Should You, In Some Other

Should you, in some other another love find,
What I did try to but failed to impress;
By Love's number, struck, in one song I bind,
That might by moon meet my pale heart profess.
Twain hearts, enjoined, together—though sweet,
With a music, by heaven,—holy ordained;
Are by night's end, split, for bodies' defeat,
In one swift-sweet note are two spirits stained.
Now but press, right palm upon tender breast
Left, not for ears—but to feel music shared;
Sadder beats, once calm, now for a touch blest,
Forever, eternal a hymn happy-paired.
Then know, if like mine, for love flutters faster,
You still own that blood in breast alabaster.

If I Am December

If I am December, then thou art May,—
We twain, for the seasons, different pain;
Myself, for my ice, and clouds cold and gray,
And you, green forever,—fresh in your reign.
Still, it was cold that night in the garden
But light, for the knowledge—Eden traversing;
As outside, the last scene, angels conversing,
Which souls to expel and which ones to pardon
O God! What sense comes from flowers commingling
The hyacinths, in and the bells brazen jingling.
But back to that night, the one when you found me
Drunk, on your beauty—the night falling through;
When the stars, and the bars, the wet wounding due,
Now nothing but perfume, a second to ground me.

My Heart—How It Leaps!

My heart—how it leaps! That sweet sound to hear,
When on some other lips your name pours forth;
Away from its owner, beside next thing dear,
Those friends that speak of you flame my torch more.
My days you without, kept busy with work
Those tasks, thought tedious once now I welcome;
To keep my mind, off, I play the dumb jerk,
Counting the time until sweet beauty's sum.
Since last you me left that place where we met
I still do go only in hopes see you there;
Those same faces, there, in same dull seats set,
But for your name to hear I would not care.
Then night, for drinks done, the lights coming on,
They still are there but you, my love, are gone.

My Heart, Trouble In

My heart, trouble in, and deep for her hid,—
Coward, for her part my fear to reveal;
To breach walls of youth, that border forbid,
Where wounds once bleeding no cold kiss can heal.
But how might I, now, my love with truth speak,
When I for my pride am in her wing pent?
In light, I have nerve, but some things I keep
Broken inside for a spoken part meant.
Still two hearts, inside, my love's breast reside,
Ever since she with her hand—talon clutched;
The one, all her own, in daylight untied,
The other one mine but with her soul untouched.
Till again, in her shadow, with eyes for her bled,
A dove I keep, dear, a friend for my bed.

An Unknown Woe Surges

An unknown woe surges, and urges me on
As my heart, for its part, cannot weight withstand;
Your own, now my all, I feel in the dawn,—
Beating, like wings for a shoreline unplanned.
But, if I told you how much I thee love,—
What good, those three words if flesh is just food?
All that air—although sweet, for you nothing prove,
Save what remains when our shadows leave nude.
When yesterday's, gone, and the next never comes
And the moon, and the stars, watch on life—the lot;
The wind, like a drug, my soul clinging numbs,
Even as flowers on my grave wilt and rot.
O, I care not! The light flown—day near done;
So precious, the night, the hour we were one.

How Sigh I With Sorrow

How sigh I with sorrow, to see the low tide,
Go out to where you my love swallow deep;
The warm ocean, vast, and waves frothy dyed,
Crashing on bones beneath, better for sleep.
When even the smallest of grains damage do,
In no time, reduce even castles to heaps;
Then what good my rack, the sea searching through,
The best pearl for finding makes one king for keeps.
But never do say my love she shall change,
One small grain from when I on here gems gazed;
Though stars, they burn out, the orbs rearrange,
She stays here stellar for mine, perfect-phrased.
So onyx, her eyes, her lips red as blood,
Then for the high tide, my spirit is mud.

Tender, Is The Day

Tender, is the day, tender still—the soft night,
When in mid June the warm zephyrs blow;
And in emerald boughs, the first summer light,
Vibrates the supple leaves sprouting below.
What more can I tell thee, but that I do love
Thee, more, than what words can possibly say;
What's a phrase, after all, but a puff of
Warm air, to garnish the last of a heavenly day.
Sweet! The green buds, that delicate hang!
About the damp lawn when the dew fallen has;
And in yonder hedge, where late the birds sang,
So too, my heart flown for light winged as,
Those angels, that dance, just ere morning breaks,
And youth, that must go its dust from flesh shakes.

Where The Buzzing Bee

Where the buzzing bee 'round clover goes,
    And those purple, globes, with nectar bulge;
So too, my love, her spirit blows
Until with lips those lips indulge.
Follow, now, the thrush—to the underbrush,
Where shadows fall in summer's rush.
In August the wind blows summer's heat,
And sends these souls with tongues to meet;
Whose tips, can taste the tendrils wet,
Moist by dusk when sunbeams set.
Or, if I can't, my love be near—
Pray breeze! Be kind her soul me send;
That from her sleeve, her perfume wend,
Then though she's there her wrist is here.
Whose rivulets, I have been told,
To her heart, lead (however cold).

'Twas There, Where Our Bodies

'Twas there, where our bodies, once twain—came one,
And fell back to earth, for ecstasy done;
And the warmth, of the light, the morning sun,
Shone on the dewdrops like glass— crystal spun.
Last time, but be not those petals that waste,—
Themselves, on themselves then fall off their stems;
Those thorns, green and stiff, left virgin, unfaced,
Sweet in themselves but die sad with their blems.
Those feathers, your pillow your perfume still hold,
Even as I awake in autumn cold;
And in them, those drawers, your diamonds and gold,
Lay right atop them those clothes not yet old.
And those roses, and lilac, I've already pressed,
Into that last book, the one that you left.

When With Thought—Mine Own End

When with thought—mine own end, I realize,--
How quick, death comes and flesh consumes;
Then the more, with my hours, what my life supplies,
I look on your bones to make sense of our tombs.
But had I, the time, and pen,—ink enough,
Might I, with true words your pure beauty write;
But my love, for my love, turns my words too rough,
For what it deserves, what is your heart white.
But take them, all—O love! Aye take here them all,—
Words, that I know far too many fall short;
To your beauty, prove, a farce all in all,
If in sad ends we both leave like a sport.
You there, in your own, with torches and worms,
And I in the other, to come to Love's terms.

Here You'll Say, Too Obscure

Here you'll say, too obscure,—that you don't under-
stand,
When at the break of day we stand;—
The shore, I mean, where time is planned,
And set in foam, and stone and sand—
O intoxication, infatuation!—
Lips, like a chalice—last libation.
And, still, that light at dawn we question,—
Those beams, (I mean) I fear to mention.
Here my heart, like a mountain inside me sinks,
When you—my lover I look on and think;
To lose you, before the sun again blinks
And stars once bright fade in skies pink.
I shall take this, cup, and fire slake,
Before in waves I drown, awake.

O Love, Should I Part

O love, should I part before my best prize,
  When Death, comes to do (what Death it just
must);
What breath, I left pent, my soul to earth cries,
Here for your body, like me soon just dust.
Should I leave, here a shade (too faint for light made)
And before, long before, your heart I can plumb;
Those depths, I shall dive, then with my lust fade,
Even as my words turn stupid and dumb.
O dust! O base lust! For my life I can't trust,
What from hereafter my soul shall become;
And what, then—O what then? When my pen is thrust,
From my only fountain, my muse taken from.
To leave, to believe, what beauty did give,
She returned twice, so we both might live.

Let Us Talk, Then Of Dust!

Let us talk, then of dust! and the ways of four winds,
And of, tombs, and the worms that only there live;
Where after, good time, none nothing there finds,
And worse, no form's there to breathe or believe.
But that slab, I'm sure is a comfortable stone
If bones, by then of marrow are bled;
The soul, for no air, to silence hath flown,
And not even shadows the next day are led.
And how true—although sad, be that note—the last,
Heard when the final hand Earth's brass bell knells;
To say, here I loved, my love to the last,
And even, beyond where the unknown dwells.
Where flesh, having turned, from hot lust to ash,
No more dying then, or hearts here to crash.

Last Night In Eden

Last night in Eden my heart hurts and swamps
My soul, as your own tempestuously beats;
Already, decided, the garden breeze prompts,—
Tempts us to do what an action depletes.
I tug on that twine, your swollen breasts on
Like a bridge, to those fig leaves twin release;
Still supple, still green, the root now rests on
And the fragrance of flowers our spirits tease.
My face leaning over, your hand reaching up,
That sweetest of fruit forbidden you pluck;
The ripest, and easiest, a low hanging sup
With a snap, seductive you bite and suck.
As the juice—(more like honey), oozes and drips,
Down off your chin to my tongue and my lips.

The Day The Third

The day the third then came to pass,
   At last! That scene upon the grass;
His lover, found him, gently sobbing,
For heart bled out inside him throbbing.
By now, the sun was well past noon,
And in the sky was Love's last moon;
Breaking, silver—sharp in June,
And playing with the stars in tune.
She approached him, there, the tree beneath,
His head bent down in dark relief;
When flashed, she did, her hidden sheath
And dropped from skin forbidden leaf.
"Dear dove," she began, then with a smile,
Cajoled his heart for just awhile;
"What for this, frown? This chin bent down?"
Then kissed him long to his pain, drown;
Then done—the deed, when lovers share,
She dried his wound with long black hair.

When Beneath You

When beneath you, still famished for knowledge I
　reach,
And tired, from painting your full beauty for;
The summer dew, we both wished, falls on the peach,
And your body, plump in the night I adore.
Then come with me, and be my love,—
This grim world, and dim, away far from;
We've the green grass, still, the blue sky above,
But autumn lurks in sorrow's gum.
Then I will, I will! This morning leave with,
You and lose all my innocence;
To the world, let rot, in rue and myth,
For what we gain, who cares—the fence.
Forever, to gaze, this night looking back,
What we did raise all others lack.

So Too

So too, when twenty-five Aprils have come,
And gone, are twenty-five Mays into June;
What of her—my first love, when in earth I'm dumb
And dead for my sorrow for leaving too soon.
In late March when walk I with friends long gone,
And sweet lovers, too—all too soon taken from;
Those footsteps I make on a snow-dusted lawn
Then look at next year to make sense, just some.
With salt drops, I think on those phrases I've kept
Cruel, for thinking too cool in youth pent;
Spending, all my time in beds better meant
For drops in true love, then with knowledge slept.
Thinking not, then nor ever, how harsh words can sever,
Warm tears melt spring ice but cold marble never.

So Now, Tit For Tat

So now, tit for tat, is love for love paid—
(Looks, also work that way front full to stack);
Then where words, decay, my heart dull and black,
I throw my wand into that sea your hand made.
Those eyes, I do love, and they—loving back,
Are windows, with which I can look on and peep;
To see, you love there, but what I then lack
Till in that bed laid, where heads fevered sleep.
But take all my love, love—aye every last drop,
From my talons, for dreaming your pure image blots;
My pen, for your seams, with ink cannot stop,
Till my hand throbbing falls off me and rots.
So warm, that last death, where waves my bones wash,
Sea, to—last sea, and wings on rocks crash.

When To Miles, I am Forced

When to miles, I am forced, her smile away from
And the distance, is counted by groans in my
throat;
The silence, turns dust, the waves never come
To carry my bark, my tempest tossed boat.
Come winds, triple whipped, with rain falling slant
And, fathoms—I know now), is my soul's surly mate;
What words, keep tight lipped, are two come I can't,
Even as ships pass like shadows too late.
And how quick, it turns sick! This ocean betwixt—
Space, where if not for my faith I would drown;
Deep, then to moan, my wraith fickle fixt,
To grovel at her foot, ankle to crown.
To prove, what is true, though distance is far,
By love she is near, to me—that last star.

Both Restless, And Weary

Both restless, and weary, the wire I traverse,—
Caught, same time eager to last beat escape;
My stars, I accept, my past I can't curse,
Sins all can do that, one's rough future shape.
That my fire, you all own from morning to moon
Should that be enough! your whole world enjoyed;
But my heart and head, too? To bleed me till June?
My feet are then cleft, last to leave destroyed.
And yet, what cheap weep to my soul searching comes,
When in my cold breast no more heat I feel;
My pate—though still wet, for sweating becomes,
The sheet on me, thrown, time to my fate seal.
O, love—I care not! As long—(as I've said),
My heart you keep, well, then happy I'm dead.

My Heart—How It Aches!

My heart—how it aches! and a dull weight descends,
My shoulders, upon and my soul drooping pins;
Full aware, of this act, my whole hell upends,
And sends my flesh packing, where no mortal wins.
By my friends, all abandoned, like old ghosts deserted,
Wanted, no longer for all of my jokes;
Those places, avoided, those others converted,
Choirs of faces the stronger world soaks.
So too, with this whole plane, base realm disgusted
If not, for my love would I've long ago fled;
To join all those, ranks, in chains old and rusted,
Bones here on earth, for pains better dead.
So sweet, those her lips, but if never kissed,
My soul is a shadow of dust never missed.

Then Utter It Not!

Then utter it not! That phrase that turns night,
To light, then flight with the colorless days;
What palms, cannot touch, the rush is the sight,
When eyes fall on feathers, others in rays.
How oft is it seen, breasts virgin do brush
Soft, in the region too far for round trips;
Then words, unreturned, the silence to crush,
Preceding the fall when standing wings clips.
Love, then let meet us on mutual ground,
Where equal hearts beat in time unison;
For too soon, for words, that cruelest of sound,
Two lungs breathe forth phrase—night one and done.
But if in fact, by the flight, my heart is proved wrong,
Then love needs no breath, so tender the throng.

Swan Songs, To Hear Them

Swan songs, to hear them why sing yours in spring
Now, when in the boughs beams dainty change;
More sweet lays, remain, where lips crimson bring,
Kisses to wan days and nights coming strange.
For but see, how you now move this last garden in
(Already, for day fled the diamonds are scattered);
Where beams, meet old dreams, the planet can't spin
What the night spilled, the light by dawn tattered—
O love! But don't waste now this time for sharp words
Lest, by the morning my hands for love fail;
Then in your arms, chaste, my bones screaming towards
Breath all I lose with my beak cold and pale.
And you, with your own, above me agape,
Ever so slightly and sweet as a grape.

Epitaphs To Write

Epitaphs to write, why chisel yours now—
Now! When so many good days you've ahead;
Soon enough, for the frost and cold on your bed,
Fingers shall brush off the snow on your brow.
Leaves of November, no one remembers,
When with scythes slashing they've fallen and flown;
Then dust, by next lust, or ash in orange embers,
Trees weep for sap lost, to face spring alone.
Beauty, whose blood through your warm veins now run,
We see in your cheek, a rose summer grown;
But by winter's gust is a web silken spun,
Then nothing is left but names on a stone.
That, and those words, that say here you once reigned,
But by winter's sting your body was drained.

Bells Of December

Bells of December, though bright none do weep,
Knowing a fire kept a flame in the hearth;
Though snows, fall on tombs, the night hath no dearth,
For beauty in bellows, warm light to keep.
So too, as it goes—smoke when censers sway,
Sweetest of incense like old brush in May;
How happy, we sing it! Beauty that stays
Long after lilac leaves, memory decays.
Those phrases that now your voice beautifies,
We love for your lung, and air on your tongue;
But time, swift and fleet, of foot and wing flies,
Then in your silence we weep for bells rung.
That place, where you lay, for duty today,
Is fit for your body but tolls for your clay.

When To Minutes, In Madness

When to minutes, in madness, my heart wounded pent,
Nights, when I still feel my own clock has time;
How might I make up? Those days for you meant,
Instead I keep my heart imprisoned, sublime.
So too, should I love—your own end precede
When, I in Death's date to that old plot go;
Be sad, for my fate, to worms frenzy feed,
But more for my questions, love never to know.
O sin! On my soul! Like a long, nagging stain
To leave thee, a lover in summer unsung;
By my own breath, held back, holding that tongue
Till time is too late, to beg for, explain.
What love, there yet speaks, when Death my fate seals,
But too deep beneath no more blood congeals.

Then Come—Let Us Not!

Then come—let us not! another night settle
Lest by the morning the day finds us bled;
These hands—for the nettled, in light cold and brittle
Or worse, for the wear—all wrinkled and dead.
O useless, this fame! This name on stone mossed,
This vessel for sinking the world, laughs and scorns.
Or like that sad bird, for light his work lost
Tender notes, for love dark dies in bloody thorns.
But should we—perchance, the happy heart seize
Horizon, that becks the soul to take flight;
For truth, find my chance, before you on knees,
For words the fear past, the waves warm and white.
To confess, there at last, what kept my heart poor,
To sigh 'pon thy breast, to breathe nevermore.

Blinded By Beauty

Blinded by beauty, my eyes inward turn
But alas! For daylight no fair I can find;
Till long journey, done, I sleep in my mind,
Where night hath no end, and Love's torches burn.
When to times my nights thy frame away from
And the silence, for distance, my spirit inhibits;
For you here---(in a sense), the sum of my wits;
In Love's depth I drown, the morning to plumb.
Those fires, thine own eyes that do shame to those stars
Torches, are mine for the tremulous night;
That I could take them with! When life with breath wars,
To look on, and take it---that comfort in sight.
O, then bright day! When thy lips two are kissed!
I'm glad for that truly but sad for those missed.

Then Kill Me Now—If Ever!

Then kill me now—if ever! With Love's vacant lips—
Cold kiss, without breath---my cup to embrace;
If after last bliss, thy hands' fragrant grips,
My last words, come easy—no more sin to face.
That once did I taste the wealth of you chaste
Forever, and sweet have I in that scent dwelt;
But that other one, treasure, left unseen, unfaced,
To heaven I go that pleasure unfelt.
That more than once have I your gems touched
Taken, to Love's height should that've been enough;
But others, there exist, like white globes unclutched,
To render my day hell, my life in love rough.
Such is it, love's first night, to last till lips bared,
Diamonds are nothing to rubies compared.

Breathe Deep, Here The Sky

Breathe deep, here the sky, luxurious peak—
Weather (whose level too high is for life);
Too spent, now to spit, too weak here to speak,
Clouds (after all), just cut like a knife.
But since some things we keep, then gathering lie
When, in that deep scene of sleep coming on;
And how might I here, heap? and how might I try?
Knowing her heart is a queen for my pawn.
And, O! What a fine piece of work is this hand!
To hold on to old sins, never to salve;
Stronger men, here have peeled, for lather they have
Spanned the breadth of flesh kept from sea to sand.
O, but to drown! In that puddle, her palm!
Then sleep, in that air, neither hot nor calm.

That Flash—I So Love

That flash—I so love, now lights up my hell
I turn to, to see it when night my crypt shows;
My love, for that look, when naked we fell,
I've placed in my book until that hard close.
That picture I painted (so many tears back)
I've kept for myself, to my own spirit please;
With that frame—for the years, too many to track,
The varnish has faded for what I can't freeze.
But far too long from them, my tomb I have faced
So much so, I fear to those sweet things forget:
That hand, I have pressed, your chin I have traced
That line of your lip, your rose red and wet.
When fires, we did light, if only so strange,
But---alas! Eyes do range, and that I can't change.

Now Love, This Doubt

Now love, this doubt: the sky is blue,
And clouds, when black a rain is due;
Doubt ice, is cold, and fire is through,
When ashes blow to somewhere new.
Doubt this: tomorrow the sun shall rise,
Again from night in eastern skies;
Doubt cool breeze comes, when summer flies
And—same breeze soothes, a teardrop dries.
Doubt time, moves fast, until it's past,
Then at the end we say at last;
Doubt seasons, move, in one straight line,
But broken clocks twice work just fine.
Doubt it! The pot that's watched never boils,
And one worm, in, the whole lot spoils;
Doubt this: the tides two times push in,
And fools in love that place rush in.
O love, all this doubt! (for none I can prove),
But this bet thy life: forever I thee love.

End Of Book One